Here's all the great literature in this grade level of *Celebrate Reading!*

BOOK A

Once Upon a Hippo

Ways of Telling Stories

Featured Poets

Beatrice Schenk de Regniers
Ed Young

The Big Blank Piece of Paper

Artists at Work

Featured Poets

Dr. Seuss
Robert Louis Stevenson
Aileen Fisher
Tomie dePaola
Alonzo Lopez

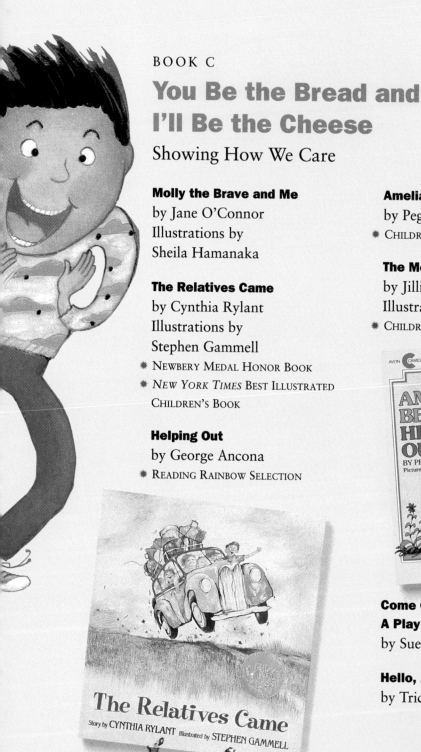

BOOK C

You Be the Bread and I'll Be the Cheese

Showing How We Care

AVON CAMELOT

AVON-0-380-53405-3 $3.50 U.S.
$4.25 CAN.

AMELIA BEDELIA HELPS OUT
BY PEGGY PARISH
Pictures by Lynn Sweat

The Relatives Came
Story by CYNTHIA RYLANT   Illustrated by STEPHEN GAMMELL

Featured Poets

Mary Ann Hoberman
Charlotte Pomerantz

BOOK E

How to Talk to Bears

And Other Tips for Success

NESSA'S FISH

HARPER
TROPHY
Under the Sunday Tree
Paintings by Mr. Amos Ferguson
...s by Eloise Greenfield

Oh No,
It's Waylon's
Birthday!

JAMES STEVENSON

BOOK F
Bathtub Voyages
Tales of Adventure

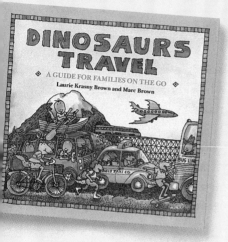

Planet of the Grown-Ups
by Gus Gedatus
Illustrations by Marc Rosenthal

The Tub People
by Pam Conrad
Illustrations by Richard Egielski
✳ CHILDREN'S CHOICE
✳ ALA NOTABLE CHILDREN'S BOOK
✳ PARENTS' CHOICE

My Dog Is Lost!
by Ezra Jack Keats
and Pat Cherr
✳ CALDECOTT MEDAL AUTHOR

The Lost Lake
by Allen Say
✳ OUTSTANDING SCIENCE TRADE BOOK

Dinosaurs Travel:
A Guide for Families on the Go
from the book by
Laurie Krasny Brown
and Marc Brown
✳ TEACHERS' CHOICE AUTHOR
AND ILLUSTRATOR

Dinosaurs, Dragonflies, and
Diamonds: All About Natural
History Museums
by Gail Gibbons
✳ OUTSTANDING SCIENCE TRADE BOOK

Featured Poets

John Ciardi
Sioux Indian Songs

Celebrate Reading!
Trade Book Library

Frog and Toad Together
by Arnold Lobel
* NEWBERY MEDAL HONOR BOOK
* ALA NOTABLE CHILDREN'S BOOK
* *SCHOOL LIBRARY JOURNAL* BEST BOOK
* READING RAINBOW SELECTION
* LIBRARY OF CONGRESS
  CHILDREN'S BOOK

The Lady with the Alligator Purse
by Nadine Bernard Westcott
* CHILDREN'S CHOICE

Henry and Mudge in Puddle Trouble
by Cynthia Rylant
* GARDEN STATE CHILDREN'S BOOK AWARD

Tyrannosaurus Was a Beast
by Jack Prelutsky
* OUTSTANDING SCIENCE TRADE BOOK

A Chair for My Mother
by Vera Williams
* CALDECOTT MEDAL HONOR BOOK
* ALA NOTABLE CHILDREN'S BOOK
* READING RAINBOW SELECTION
* BOSTON GLOBE-HORN BOOK AWARD

Paul Bunyan
by Steven Kellogg
* READING RAINBOW SELECTION

Big & Little Book Library

Rockabye Crocodile
by Jose Aruego and Ariane Dewey

Putting on a Play
by Caroline Feller Bauer
Illustrations by Cyd Moore
* CHRISTOPHER AWARD AUTHOR

We Are Best Friends
by Aliki
* CHILDREN'S CHOICE AUTHOR

Fables from Around the World
retold by Lily Toy Hong, Carmen Tafolla, Tom Paxton, Joseph Bruchac, and Nancy Ross Ryan

Wings: A Tale of Two Chickens
by James Marshall
* CHILDREN'S CHOICE AUTHOR
* PARENTS' CHOICE AUTHOR
* ALA NOTABLE BOOK AUTHOR

Is There Life in Outer Space?
by Franklyn M. Branley
Illustrations by Don Madden
* READING RAINBOW BOOK

Bathtub Voyages

Tales of Adventure

Once Upon a Hippo
The Big Blank Piece of Paper
You Be the Bread and I'll Be the Cheese
Why Does Water Wiggle?
How to Talk to Bears
Bathtub Voyages

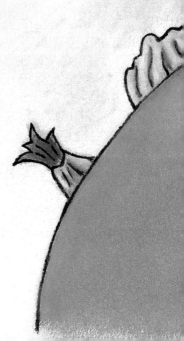

About the Cover Artist
Lee Lee Brazeal lives out in the country near a small
town that has a gas station and a post office. She rides
her show jumper "Teddy Ruxbin" every day. She also has
a toy poodle and a Welsh corgi named Duder Bud Dog.

ISBN 0-673-82093-9

1995 printing
Copyright © 1993
Scott, Foresman and Company, Glenview, Illinois
All Rights Reserved.
Printed in the United States of America.

Acknowledgments appear on page 144.

12345678910VHJ999897969594

Bathtub Voyages

Tales of Adventure

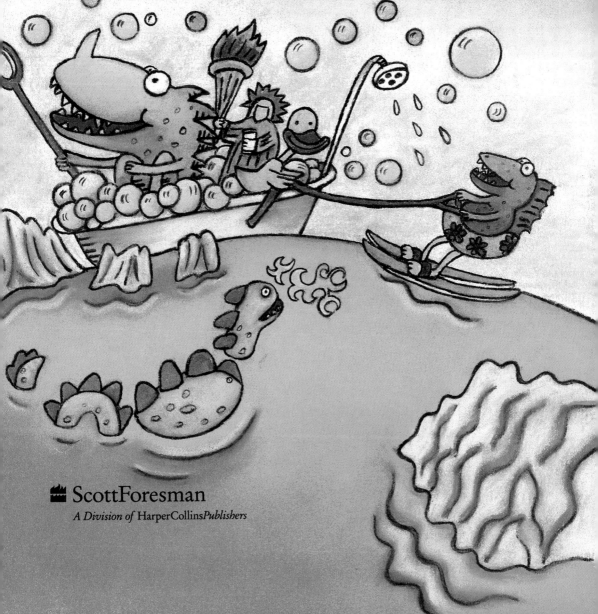

ScottForesman

A Division of HarperCollinsPublishers

CONTENTS

Just My Imagination

Student Resources

My dog is lost!

EZRA JACK KEATS and PAT CHERR

Juanito was miserable.
Only two days before, on his eighth birthday,
he and his family had arrived in New York,
all the way from Puerto Rico.
Now he was in a new home,
with no friends to talk to.
For Juanito spoke only Spanish.
And, to make him feel even lonelier . . .

. . . his dog was lost.
Juanito's dog had been his best friend
ever since he could remember.
He was a Puerto Rican dog
so he understood only Spanish.
He had been gone since yesterday.
Juanito missed him so much
that he decided to look for his dog
all by himself.

He tried
not to cry
as he looked
in the grocery . . .

. . . the school playground . . .

. . . the movie lobby.

8

Would he never see his dog again?

He ran to the butcher shop . . .

. . . to the laundromat . . .

. . . to the subway entrance.
The busy streets frightened him.
The words the people spoke sounded strange.

Suddenly he saw a big stone building
with wide glass windows.
He read the sign on the window.
There were people inside who spoke his language.
Would they be able to help him?

BANK OF

AQUÍ SE HABLA ESPAÑOL

10

"Mi perro se ha perdido," he said.
Mr. Hernández, the bank teller, understood Juanito.
He changed the Spanish words into English
and wrote them on a piece of paper to help Juanito.

MY DOG
IS LOST

Again Juanito went out to the street.
What great, tall buildings!
So many people and so many cars!
They frightened Juanito,
but his love for his dog made him brave.
If he had to,
he would search this strange, new city
from beginning to end.

He held tight to the piece of paper
and started again to look for his dog.

13

Juanito walked to Chinatown.
He showed the paper to Lily and Kim Lee.
Lily pointed to the crayons
in her little brother's hand
and asked, "What color is your dog?"
Juanito tugged at his brightly colored shirt.

4

Little Kim asked,
"What kind of hair does your dog have?"
He pulled at his own shiny black hair.
Juanito pointed at a little lady in a big fur coat.

16

peludo!

They shook their heads.
"We haven't seen a red, shaggy dog,"
said Lily and Kim Lee, "but we'll help you look."

They walked to a part of the city
called Little Italy. There they met Angelo.
He made believe he was a dog. He barked and ran.
"Does your dog run like this?"

¡zambo!

Juanito bent his legs to show how his dog ran.

"I want to see a dog that runs like that,"
said Angelo. "I'll help you look."

Juanito and Lily, Kim and Angelo
walked to Park Avenue.
They met the twins, Sally and Susie,
and told them all about the lost dog.
Sally measured with her hands.
"Is your dog large or small?"

¡grande!

Juanito stretched his arms
as far apart as they could go.

"What kind of eyes does your dog have?"
asked Susie, pointing to her own.

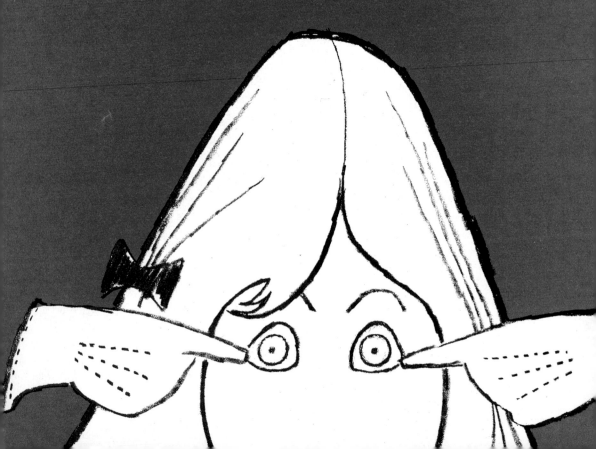

Juanito made his eyes look very tiny.

¡pequeños!

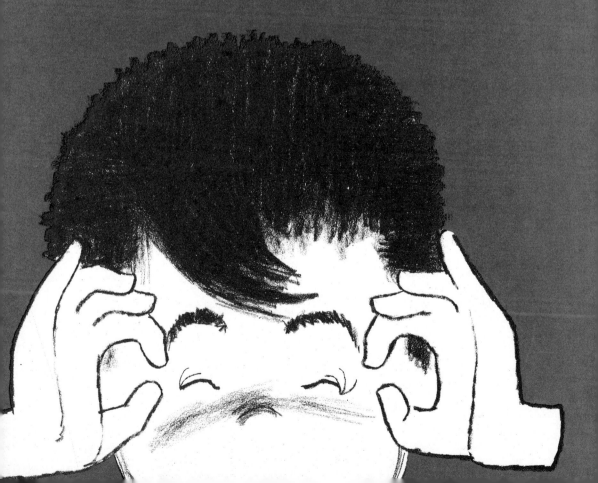

They rode on a bus to Harlem,
where they met Billy and Bud.
"Have you seen a lost dog that's red,
shaggy, bowlegged, and big,
with little eyes?" they asked.
"No," said Billy.
He pointed to the name on his sweater.
Bud did the same, too.
"What is your dog's name?" Billy asked.

¡PEPITO!

As he said the name
Juanito could hold back
his tears no longer.
"Don't give up," said Billy.
"We're all with you.
   We'll help you look."

25

Then they all ran with Juanito
to help him find his dog.
They ran for blocks. They looked everywhere.
They looked and looked and looked.
But there was no sign of a dog named Pepito
that was red, shaggy, bowlegged, and big,
and had little eyes.
"I'm tired," said Lily Lee.
"Me, too," said Kim Lee.
"It's getting late," said Angelo.
"I'm hungry," said Sally.
"We'd better go home," said Susie.
"I wish I could speak Spanish," said Billy,
"so I could explain to him."

And then . . .
they met a policeman.
Juanito showed him the note.
The policeman asked,
"What sort of dog is he?"

WOOF
WOOF

27

RED!

BOW-
LEGGED!

MY DOG IS LOST

"Of course!" said the policeman.

¡jau-jau!

"We've been looking for you, too!"

¡perrito mio!

"He's found!" yelled Lily.

"He's found!" yelled Kim.

"He sure is bowlegged," said Angelo.

"He's nice," said Sally.

"I like him," said Susie.

"Hurray!" shouted Billy.

And Pepito said,

¡jau-jau!

Juanito was too happy to say a word.

He and his new friends took Pepito home.

Aquí se habla español. ....Spanish spoken here.

Mi perro se ha perdido. ....My dog is lost.

rojo .... red

peludo ....shaggy

zambo ....bowlegged

grande ....big

pequeños ....little

perrito mío ....my puppy

jau-jau ....bow-wow

Woof
Woof

Thinking About It

1. ¡Pepito! Did you think Juanito would find him? Do you think that Pepito was looking for Juanito? Tell why you think that way. What will you say to them?

2. *¡Jau-jau!* Pepito understands Spanish. Will he learn English too? Why or why not? If he does learn English, who will teach him?

3. Now *your* dog is lost. Or your best friend's dog is lost. No one understands your language! Think of some different ways to tell people about the lost dog without using language.

Another Book by Ezra Jack Keats
In *Regards to the Man in the Moon*, Louie and his friends take a trip into space. Is it real or imaginary?

THE LOST LAKE

WRITTEN AND ILLUSTRATED BY

ALLEN SAY

I went to live with Dad last summer.

Every day he worked in his room from
morning to night, sometimes on weekends,
too. Dad wasn't much of a talker, but when
he was busy he didn't talk at all.

I didn't know anybody in the city, so I
stayed home most of the time. It was too hot
to play outside anyway. In one month I
finished all the books I'd brought and grew
tired of watching TV.

One morning I started cutting pictures
out of old magazines, just to be doing
something. They were pictures of mountains
and rivers and lakes, and some showed
people fishing and canoeing. Looking at
them made me feel cool, so I pinned them
up in my room.

Dad didn't notice them for two days.
When he did, he looked at them one by one.

"Nice pictures," he said.

"Are you angry with me, Dad?" I asked, because he saved old magazines for his work.

"It's all right, Luke," he said. "I'm having this place painted soon anyway."

He thought I was talking about the marks I'd made on the wall.

That Saturday Dad woke me up early in the morning and told me we were going camping! I was wide awake in a second. He gave me a pair of brand-new hiking boots to try out. They were perfect.

In the hallway I saw a big backpack and a knapsack all packed and ready to go.

"What's in them, Dad?" I asked.

"Later," he said. "We have a long drive ahead of us."

In the car I didn't ask any more questions because Dad was so grumpy in the morning.

"Want a sip?" he said, handing me his mug. He'd never let me drink coffee before. It had lots of sugar in it.

"Where are we going?" I finally asked.

"We're off to the Lost Lake, my lad."

"How can you lose a lake?"

"No one's found it, that's how." Dad was smiling! "Grandpa and I used to go there a long time ago. It was our special place, so don't tell any of your friends."

"I'll never tell," I promised. "How long are we going to stay there?"

"Five days, maybe a week."

"We're going to sleep outside for a whole week?"

"That's the idea."

"Oh, boy!"

We got to the mountains in the afternoon.

"It's a bit of a hike to the lake, son,"
Dad said.

"I don't mind," I told him. "Are there any
fish in the lake?"

"Hope so. We'll have to catch our dinner,
you know."

"You didn't bring any food?"

"Of course not. We're going to live like true outdoorsmen."

"Oh . . ."

Dad saw my face and started to laugh. He must have been joking. I didn't think we were going very far anyway, because Dad's pack was so heavy I couldn't even lift it.

Well, Dad was like a mountain goat. He went straight up the trail, whistling all the while. But I was gasping in no time. My knapsack got very heavy and I started to fall behind.

Dad stopped for me often, but he wouldn't let me take off my pack. If I did I'd be too tired to go on, he said.

It was almost suppertime when we got to the lake.

The place reminded me of the park near Dad's apartment. He wasn't whistling or humming anymore.

"Welcome to the *Found* Lake," he muttered from the side of his mouth.

"What's wrong, Dad?"

"Do you want to camp with all these people around us?"

"I don't mind."

"Well, I do!"

"Are we going home?"

"Of course not!"

He didn't even take off his pack. He just turned and started to walk away.

Soon the lake was far out of sight.

Then it started to rain. Dad gave me a
poncho and it kept me dry, but I wondered
where we were going to sleep that night. I
wondered what we were going to do for
dinner. I wasn't sure about camping anymore.

I was glad when Dad finally stopped and set up the tent. The rain and wind beat against it, but we were warm and cozy inside. And Dad had brought food. For dinner we had salami and dried apricots.

"I'm sorry about the lake, Dad," I said.

He shook his head. "You know something, Luke? There aren't any secret places left in the world anymore."

"What if we go very far up in the mountains? Maybe we can find our own lake."

"There are lots of lakes up here, but that one was special."

"But we've got a whole week, Dad."

"Well, why not? Maybe we'll find a lake that's not on the map."

"Sure, we will!"

We started early in the morning. When
the fog cleared we saw other hikers ahead of
us. Sure enough, Dad became very glum.

"We're going cross-country, partner," he said.

"Won't we get lost?"

"A wise man never leaves home without
his compass."

So we went off the trail. The hills went
on and on. The mountains went on and on.
It was kind of lonesome. It seemed as if Dad
and I were the only people left in the world.

And then we hiked into a big forest.

At noontime we stopped by a creek and
ate lunch and drank ice-cold water straight
from the stream. I threw rocks in the water,
and fish, like shadows, darted in the pools.

"Isn't this a good place to camp, Dad?"

"I thought we were looking for our lake."

"Yes, right . . ." I mumbled.

The forest went on and on.

"I don't mean to scare you, son," Dad said. "But we're in bear country. We don't want to surprise them, so we have to make a lot of noise. If they hear us, they'll just go away."

What a time to tell me! I started to shout as loudly as I could. Even Dad wouldn't be able to beat off bears. I thought about those people having fun back at the lake. I thought about the creek, too, with all those fish in it. That would have been a fine place to camp. The Lost Lake hadn't been so bad either.

It was dark when we got out of the forest.
We built a fire and that made me feel better.
Wild animals wouldn't come near a fire.
Dad cooked beef stroganoff and it was
delicious.

Later it was bedtime. The sleeping bag
felt wonderful. Dad and I started to count

the shooting stars, then I worried that maybe we weren't going to find our lake.

"What are you thinking about, Luke?" Dad asked.

"I didn't know you could cook like that," I said.

Dad laughed. "That was only freeze-dried stuff. When we get home, I'll cook you something really special."

"You know something, Dad? You seem like a different person up here."

"Better or worse?"

"A lot better."

"How so?"

"You talk more."

"I'll have to talk more often, then."

That made me smile. Then I slept.

Dad shook me awake. The sun was just coming up, turning everything all gold and orange and yellow. And there was the lake, right in front of us.

For a long time we watched the light change on the water, getting brighter and brighter. Dad didn't say a word the whole time. But then, I didn't have anything to say either.

After breakfast we climbed a mountain and saw our lake below us. There wasn't a sign of people anywhere. It really seemed as if Dad and I were all alone in the world.

I liked it just fine.

THINKING ABOUT IT

1. Step into the illustrations. If you were with Luke and his father, which pictures would you like to be in? What would you say and do?

2. Be Luke and tell someone about your camping trip. How will you do this to make it most interesting?

3. Do you have a "lost lake"? Tell about going somewhere with someone you like. Make it an experience you'll remember happily when you are one hundred years old.

ANOTHER BOOK ABOUT A LAKE

Does Muskrat Lake really have any muskrats? That's one thing Pearl and Rosemary want to know in *Weekend at Muskrat Lake* by Nicki Weiss.

Songs of the Horse Society

Daybreak
appears
when
a horse
neighs

Friend
my horse
flies like a bird
as it runs

SIOUX INDIAN SONGS

54

DINOSAURS
ON THE ROAD

Laurie Krasny Brown
and Marc Brown

Do you ever wish you could climb a mountain,

fly through the air,

or ride around town in a long limousine?

Every time you leave home, whether to travel

around the world,

or around the block,
get ready for an
adventure!

GETTING READY FOR A TRIP

Books and maps can help you learn about a new place before you go there.

You may not be able to take your pets with you, but someone else will take good care of them.

If you take the addresses of friends and relatives, you can write to them while you're away.

Find out about the
weather where you're
going and choose clothes
that will be good to wear.

Only pack a few toys,
games, books, and tapes.
Small, light, and sturdy
things travel best.

Remember one or two
favorite companions.

And don't forget these!

Wherever you're headed,

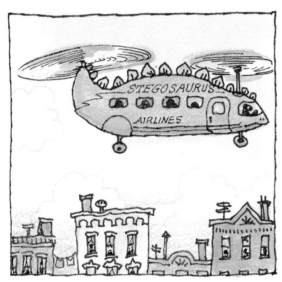

getting there can be part of the fun!

Walking lets you stop and see the sights.

You may meet other travelers along the way.

You can hike on a trail where almost no one ever goes.

And your body is all that you need!

YOUR OWN WHEELS

Bicycles and skateboards are faster than walking.

You're the driver! It's up to you to know the rules of the road.

Keep your bike or board in good working order, so you're all set to ride anytime.

With your own set of wheels, you can go most anywhere!

You and your family can go biking together.

Sometimes you have to pedal hard to get where you're going,

but downhill you get a free ride!

Cars will take you on all kinds of roads. Riding on the highways is fastest!

Driving on back roads is slower but you see more.

You and your family can go wherever or whenever you want.

You can bring along lots of your things—if you have room!

You and your family can play word games while you ride. You can take turns reading road signs or looking at different license plates.

It feels good to get out and stretch your legs from time to time.

Switching seats will give you different views.

If you have a cassette player, you can bring your favorite tapes.

In some cities riding underground in a subway is the fastest way to travel.

On a bus you can see what's going on outside. A tour bus driver will point out the sights.

On a subway or bus you must pay a fare to ride.

Subways and buses make many stops. Don't forget to watch for yours!

You can buy a ticket for
the train at the station.
Look at the signs for your
track and departure time.

All aboard!

Taking the train is a great way to see new places!

On most trains, you can sit facing forward or backward.

The conductor announces each stop the train makes. You can follow along with a timetable.

Trains don't have to stop until they pull into a station.

The train stops at many stations so passengers can get on and off.

Boats can take you across an ocean,

down rapids,

or to an island in the middle of a lake.

Some ferryboats carry cars and trucks as well as passengers.

It's smart to wear a life jacket in a small boat.

To travel on some boats, *you* have to do all the work!

FLYING IN PLANES

At the airport an agent looks at your ticket, checks your luggage, and assigns you a seat on the plane.

Airport security makes sure no one carries anything dangerous or illegal on the plane.

You can bring a small bag on most planes and stow it under or above your seat. Buckle up!

Take off!

As the plane climbs higher, things below look smaller and smaller.

You'll fly up above the clouds!

If taking off makes your ears hurt, keep swallowing, chew gum, or suck on candy. When the "Fasten Seatbelts" sign goes off, you can stretch or move around. Pay attention to instructions about what to do in an emergency.

Every seat has special buttons and equipment. You can turn on your overhead light to read.

When you land, the plane puts down its wheels and taxis to the gate. You're back on the ground!

No matter where you travel, it will be different from home.

When you explore a new place, you might be surprised at what you find.

Here's your chance to try all kinds of new things!

Bring maps and guidebooks with you, and ask for directions if you get lost.

You may make new friends on your trip.

You can learn how others like to live.

Some places you visit will give you a chance to speak a new language.

1. Dinosaurs travel? Well, dinosaurs travel in books. What about you? Tell about your most unforgettable trip. If you tell the dinosaur family about it, what part of your trip will you tell about the most?

2. What are the three most important travel tips in *Dinosaurs Travel*? Why do you think so?

3. Congratulations! You have won a dream vacation! You can go anywhere in the world! Where will you go? How will you get there? What will you do while you are there?

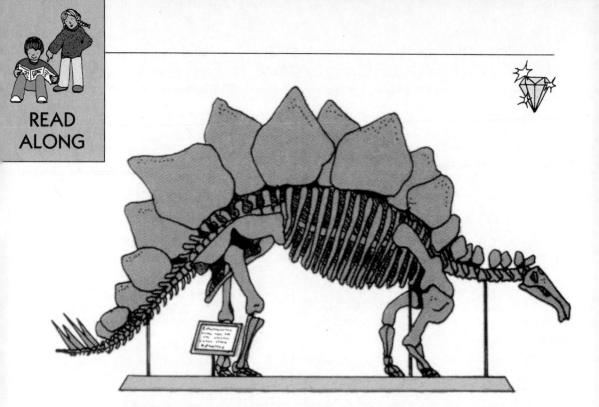

Dinosaurs, Dragonflies & Diamonds

ALL ABOUT NATURAL HISTORY MUSEUMS

BY GAIL GIBBONS

Millions of dinosaur bones, big and small dragonflies, glittering diamonds under one roof! Natural history museums have many exhibits to look at and huge collections of stored objects to study. Their subject: the history of nature and human beings.

The first natural history museum in the United States was formed in 1773 in South Carolina. The people of that state were expected to provide the collections. They were asked to give ". . . the various fossils, minerals and ores, the different soils, clays, marles, stones, sands and shells. . . ."

There are now many natural history museums in the United States, and in the rest of the world as well. Some are small. Others are huge. Visitors from all over the world come to the museums. There is much to see.

There are exhibits of birds, plants,
fishes, and wild animals. Some of the
exhibits are called habitat groups. They
show the way the animals look in their
natural homes.

There are displays about the history of human beings, about gems, about bugs, and more.

Dinosaurs! They lived millions of years ago. Visitors stare up at the huge standing skeletons.

Most of the exhibits at natural history museums are there all the time. They are called permanent exhibits.

But often there are special shows. They are called temporary exhibits. GOLD! Banners advertise the special event. Gold nuggets shine in their display cases.

A movie about the California gold rush appears on the screen in the background. Look! A gold bar and lots of gold jewelry. Gold everywhere!

A group of visitors listens to their tour
guide. "This pottery is about four thousand
years old." Another tour group of
schoolchildren is close behind.

Natural history museums often have gift shops. Some visitors buy books. Others buy souvenirs to remind them of their visit.

Throughout the year, the museums present special lectures and activities for visitors to attend. Some people sign up for trips with museum tour guides. Often the trips are to faraway places.

Scientists come to natural history
museums to study the vast collections.
Behind closed doors, they take their notes.
They find drawers and drawers of stones,
animal bones, Indian clothing, beetles. . . .
Millions and millions of objects are stored here.

Behind the scenes, it takes many workers for the museums to run smoothly. Some workers are busy labeling, tagging, and recording all of the many stored items.

Staff scientists work in their labs, making new discoveries about nature and people.

Museums often create new exhibits, too.

How a New Rattlesnake Exhibit Is Made

The museum sends a curator—the person in charge of the exhibit—and artists on an expedition.

curator

background artist

The background artist paints what the location looks like.

foreground
artist

The foreground artist collects plants,
rocks, and sand.

A zoo has donated several dead rattlesnakes to the museum. The sculptor will make plastic snakes for the exhibit.

sculptor

frame

1. First, a snake is pinned in position.

2. Rubber is poured into the frame.

3. When the rubber hardens, the snake is removed.

rubber mold

writer

4. Then, liquid plastic is poured into the mold.

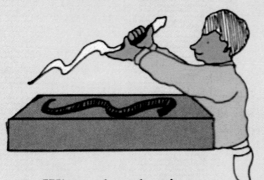

5. When the plastic hardens, the exhibit snake is removed.

6. When all three plastic snakes are ready, they are carefully painted.

The background is painted.

papier-mâché rock

The plants here are not real. They were made to look like plants brought back to the museum.

Everything is put in place.

The rattlesnakes look alive in their natural setting.

Other workers handle museum business.
Many are there to assist visitors and
answer their questions.

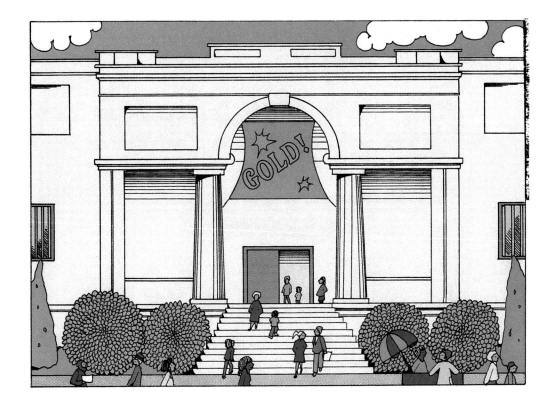

Natural history museums are where to
go to have fun, to make new discoveries
. . . and to see the dinosaurs!

LEARNING ABOUT
Natural History
Museums

BY GAIL GIBBONS

Gail Gibbons [signature]

When I was a child, I enjoyed visiting natural history museums. But I didn't think of writing a book about them until I was working on two other books, *Dinosaurs* and *Prehistoric Animals*.

To do my research for those books, I went to the American Museum of Natural History in New York City. I talked to people who knew a lot about dinosaurs and prehistoric animals.

While I was there, I became fascinated with the museum itself. How did a natural history museum work?

What did it have on display? How did museums find
things for their displays? That's when I decided to
write a book about natural history museums.

When I started my new book, I did the research
first. I asked the people who worked at the American
Museum of Natural History to tell me about their
work. I looked for helpful books in the library at
the museum.

I did have one problem. I couldn't visit some of the rooms at the museum, because only workers were allowed inside them. But I wanted my book to explain what happened in *every* part of the museum. How could I find out what I needed to know?

Luckily for me, the museum had photographs and films that showed what happened in the rooms I couldn't visit. I found photos that showed how millions of objects are stored at the museum. I saw how the scientists worked in their labs. I even saw an old film that showed how dinosaur skeletons were put back together. The photos and films helped me draw my illustrations.

After I wrote the book, I asked someone at the museum to check all the facts in it. Since people read my books for information, I want everything to be correct. If I make a mistake, I know someone will call me and tell me my book is wrong! So before a book is printed, I always make sure it has been carefully checked.

I enjoyed writing and illustrating *Dinosaurs, Dragonflies and Diamonds*. I hope you enjoyed finding out how *I* learned all about natural history museums.

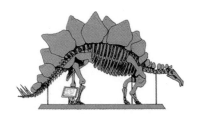

Thinking About It

1. Take time to be curious. Find three things in
   Dinosaurs, Dragonflies and Diamonds that you
   are curious about. Make up some questions you
   would ask people in the museum about these things.

2. *Dinosaurs, Dragonflies and Diamonds* is
   nonfiction, not a story. Tell why.

3. Oh my! Someone from the planet Xcxpfgmz is
   here. She wants to take back a display that shows
   your classroom to the creatures of Xcxpfgmz.
   Help her plan the display for her planet.

ANOTHER BOOK BY GAIL GIBBONS

In *Dinosaurs,* you'll find out why some of these
"terrible lizards" weren't really terrible at all.

Planet of the GROWN-UPS

by GUS GEDATUS
Illustrations by MARC ROSENTHAL

Cast

EARTHLINGS *(people from Earth)*

☐ Tasha   ☐ Pat

☐ Anna   ☐ Other Children

☐ Louis

ZARLOIDS *(people from Planet Zarlo)*

☐ Zegna

☐ Policeperson

☐ Janitor

Props

☐ A desk

☐ A stack of paper "schedules" lying on top of the desk

☐ A chair

☐ A large cardboard box decorated to look like a computer

Special Effects

☐ Make buzzes, whirs, hums, and clicks for the sounds of the computer.

☐ Switch the classroom lights on and off to show the computer is working very hard.

Costumes

☐ Tasha wears regular clothes.

☐ All other characters wear large paper bags or large shirts worn backwards.

☐ The Policeperson also wears a badge.

☐ The Janitor carries a feather duster, and is missing one shoe.

(Setting: The scene is the computer room on Planet Zarlo. Zegna is asleep in a chair, snoring. Tasha enters.)

Tasha: *(loudly)* Hello! Hello! Is anyone here?

Zegna: What? *(Zegna wakes up suddenly.)* Yes— over here!

Tasha: *(confused)* Where am I?

Zegna: You're on the planet Zarlo. I'm the Chief Handshaker. *(Zegna grabs Tasha's hand and shakes it.)* My name is Zegna.

Tasha: Zegna! That's a funny name.

Zegna: It is not! You Earthlings can be so rude!

Tasha: I'm sorry. *(She looks around.)* How did I get here? I was at a carnival.

Zegna: Do you remember the "Space Explorers" ride?

Tasha: Oh, yes. The sign said, "Visit Planet Zarlo! It's a grown-up thing to do!" I waited a long time to get on that ride.

Zegna: Well, it brought you here. Surprise! *(Zegna goes over to the computer.)* Now, what kind of job would you like, Tasha?

Tasha: Job? I can't have a job. I'm just a kid.

Zegna: Not anymore. Everyone here is grown-up, with a job.

Tasha: Really? Neat! Grown-ups have all the fun! (*Louis, Pat, Anna, and other Earthlings enter. Zegna shakes their hands.*)

Tasha: Louis, Pat, Anna—everybody! You're here, too. You got on that ride right before I did.

Louis: We came to pick up our work schedules.

Tasha: Are you grown-ups now?

Louis: Oh, yes. I'm a plumber.

Pat: I'm a bus driver.

Anna: I'm a doctor.

Zegna: Everyone works on Zarlo.

Tasha: You're not children anymore?

Louis: I'm twenty-four years old now.

Pat: I'll be twenty-five next week.

Anna: I'm getting married soon. (*All pick up work schedules.*)

Zegna: On Zarlo, we have a special computer program that turns children into grown-ups right away.

Louis: They got tired of hearing kids say, "I want to be grown up."

Pat: Planet Zarlo doesn't have to build playgrounds or schools or amusement parks like Planet Earth.

Anna: We work all the time—just like grown-ups.

Tasha: That doesn't sound like much fun. Do you like it?

Louis: *(He scratches his head.)* Sort of.

Pat: *(frowning)* I think so.

Anna: *(quietly)* Sometimes. *(Tasha looks like she doesn't believe them.)*

Louis: Well, see you later. I have to fix a kitchen sink. *(He exits.)*

Pat: There are people waiting for the bus. *(Pat exits.)*

Anna: I have to look at a broken leg. *(Anna and other Earthlings exit.)*

Zegna: Now, Tasha, what job shall the computer give you? Shall I make you a lion tamer?

Tasha: Oh, no!

Zegna: You *do* want to be a grown-up, don't you?

Tasha: I don't know. *(to herself)* What am I going to do? I don't want to be a grown-up here, and I don't think the other kids do either. How can I get us back home? . . . Oh, I know! *(She smiles, and talks to Zegna.)* I want to be a computer expert.

Zegna: Very good! Now stand by the computer, with your hands on top. *(Zegna types into the computer. It makes loud noises, and the classroom lights blink off and on.)* There—that didn't hurt, did it?

Tasha: Oh, no. *(She starts typing into the computer. It makes more loud noises, and the lights blink off and on again.)*

Zegna: What are you doing? You can't change the computer!

Tasha: I'm the expert now, so let me work! *(She keeps typing.)* If I make just a few changes, I'll be able to see all over the planet with this computer!

Policeperson: *(coming in)* Zegna, my police whistle won't blow anymore. I could cry! Boo-hoo-hoo!

Janitor: *(coming in)* What's going on? My vacuum cleaner ate my shoe and then stopped running!

Zegna: It must be this Earthling! She changed the computer and everything on Zarlo is getting mixed up!

Tasha: *(pointing at the computer screen)* I can see Pat in the bus—and there's Anna and Louis and the others. I'll have Pat pick them up in the bus. *(Tasha exits.)*

Zegna: *(to the Policeperson)* Don't just stand there—bring her back!

Policeperson: How can I bring her back without my whistle? *(The Policeperson starts yelling.)* Yoohoo, oh, yoohoo! *(The Policeperson exits.)*

Zegna: *(to the Janitor)* Do you know anything about computers?

Janitor: I can't think without my shoe! *(The Janitor starts hopping on one foot.)*

Zegna: Maybe I can do something. *(Zegna tries to type, but the computer makes angry noises and the lights blink. Tasha returns with the other Earthlings and the Policeperson.)*

Tasha: You can't stop us, Zegna. We're going home. *(She types at the computer.)*

Policeperson: *(crying)* Oh, I need my whistle! Boo-hoo-hoo!

Louis: At first I liked being here, but now I hope we can go back home.

Pat: Me too! I don't want to have a job yet.

Anna: I want to go to school and have fun—like a kid!

Tasha: Come here, everybody, and put your hands on top of the computer. *(The Earthlings all put their hands on the computer.)*

Zegna: You'll never make it back to Earth!

Tasha: Watch us! *(The computer makes happy noises, and the lights blink very quickly. The Earthlings twirl around, and exit. The lights go out. The Zarloids exit, taking the computer, the desk, and the chair with them. Tasha and the other Earthlings enter. The lights go back on.)*

Louis: Hurray! We're back at the carnival—on Earth!

Anna: And we're kids again! I'm so happy—I'm not ready to be a grown-up yet.

Pat: Driving a bus in all that traffic was horrible!

All: Thanks, Tasha!

Louis: What should we do now?

Tasha: Well, we could go on the "Space Explorers" ride again.

All: No way! *(They all laugh.)*

THE END

THINKING ABOUT IT

1. Being a grown-up on Zarlo isn't much fun. How do you feel about becoming a grown-up? What do you think you'll like and dislike about it? Why?

2. In the play, how do the children feel about being grown-ups? Why do they feel that way? How do you know?

3. What if Tasha tries another carnival ride? What might happen to her?

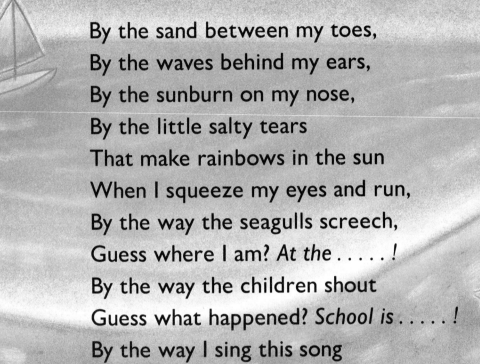

Summer Song

By the sand between my toes,
By the waves behind my ears,
By the sunburn on my nose,
By the little salty tears
That make rainbows in the sun
When I squeeze my eyes and run,
By the way the seagulls screech,
Guess where I am? *At the* . . . . . !
By the way the children shout
Guess what happened? *School is* . . . . . !
By the way I sing this song
Guess if summer lasts too long:
You must answer Right or . . . . . !

—John Ciardi

BY PAM CONRAD

ILLUSTRATIONS BY RICHARD EGIELSKI

The Tub People stood in a line all day on the
edge of the bathtub. There were seven of them,
and they always stood in the same order—the
father, the mother, the grandmother, the
doctor, the policeman, the child and the dog.

They were made out of wood, and their faces
were very plain. They could smile or frown, or
cry or laugh. Sometimes they would even wink
at each other, but it hardly showed.

The father of the Tub People liked to play
sea captain. He would take the mother, the
grandmother and the child for a ride on the
floating soap. The others stood on the edge of
the tub and waved. Once in a while the child of
the Tub People would slide off the soap into
the warm bath.

"Help! Help!"

And the captain would rescue him.

"We're coming! We're coming!"

The policeman and the doctor liked to have water races, bobbing from one end of the tub to the other. The child would cheer. The grandmother would say, "Hush! You're very noisy."

When bathtime was over, the Tub People always lined up along the edge of the bathtub— the father, the mother, the grandmother, the doctor, the policeman, the child and the dog.

But one evening the bathwater began rushing
down the drain before they were lined up,
pulling all the Tub People this way and that.
The soap danced over to the drain, turning and
turning at the top of a whirlpool. Standing on
the soap, getting dizzier and dizzier, was the
child of the Tub People.

"Help! Help!"

But this time his father could not save him.

And the Tub Child disappeared down the drain without a sound.

The Tub Mother pressed her face to the grating. She looked and looked for her Tub Child. But she could not see him.

Later that night the Tub People lined up on the edge of the tub, just the six of them. The soap was soft and back in the soap dish. The washcloth made a lonely dripping sound as it hung from the faucet.

The Tub People felt very sad.

The next night the six Tub People climbed onto the washcloth raft. They called and called for their Tub Child. Of course, they knew exactly where their child had gone. But somehow they felt comforted by calling for him.

"Honey, where are you? Come home now. Please come back." But he did not answer.

Every evening the Tub People continued to float in the bathwater. But in time they stopped calling.

And they never winked at each other anymore.

Then an unusual thing happened. The bathwater began going down the drain slower and slower.

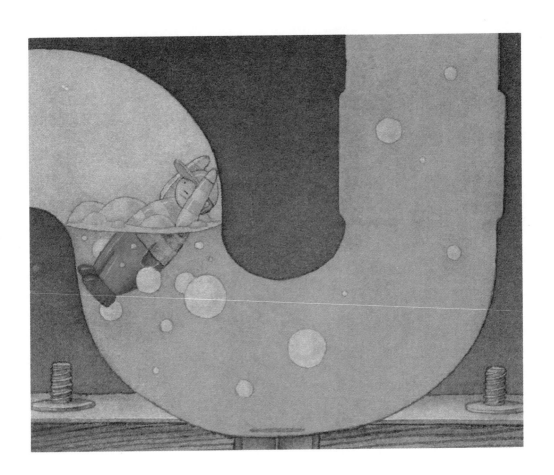

Big people came and peered into the tub. "What's the matter with the tub drain?" they asked. They filled the room with deep voices and blocked the light.

"What's the matter with the tub drain?"

The Tub People stood woodenly in their line. If they could have spoken, they would have shouted out what a terrible drain that was, and how it had sucked away their little Tub Child. But they were silent.

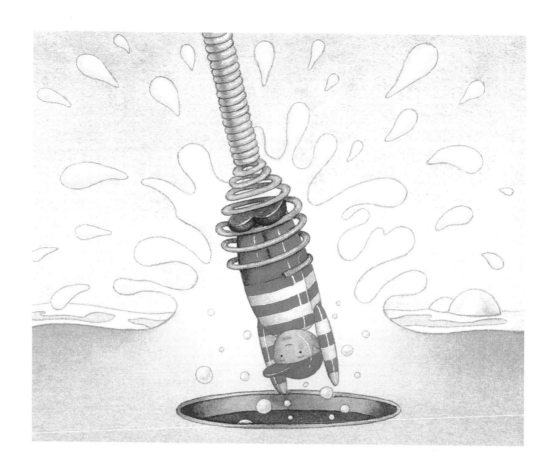

That afternoon, a big man came and pried off the drain cover, grunting as he worked. He shone a light down the drain and frowned. Then he pushed in a long wire and jiggled it up and down. Up and down.

"Come home now," the grandmother whispered.

And out of the drain popped the little Tub Child, wet and tired.

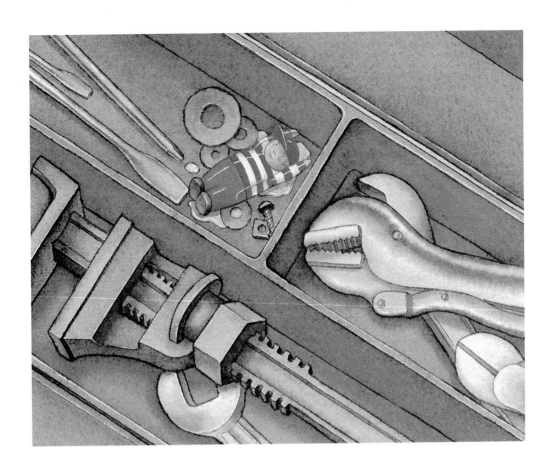

The Tub People stood in a line, quietly watching. One by one they smiled—the father, the mother, the grandmother, the doctor, the policeman and the dog. And the Tub Mother had little soapy tears running down her wooden cheeks.

But the big man did not look at them. He tossed the Tub Child into his toolbox, shut it with a click and left.

The Tub People waited for bathtime, hoping their Tub Child would come back.

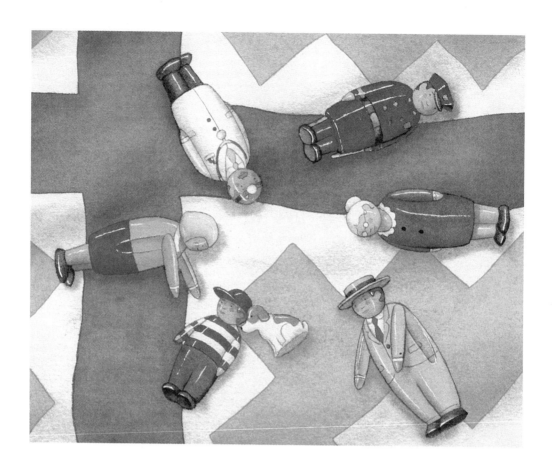

But bathtime never came. It grew later and later, and still they waited, worrying all the while.

Finally, when they felt they could wait no longer, they were lifted up and carefully carried into a new room and gently placed on a large, soft bed! It seemed just like the water to them, except that it was dry and very firm.

And there were seven of them once again! The Tub Dog knocked his little wooden head against the Tub Child's head, and very quietly they all laughed.

There was a thick quilt on the bed, and when it was all bunched up, they would go mountain climbing. The father liked to be the leader, and he would lead them up one side of the mountain, and then they would all tumble easily down the other.

The grandmother liked to hide under the pillow and have everyone come find her. The Tub Child liked to fall off the edge and have his father rescue him.

Each night when the lights went out, they
lined up along the windowsill, just as they had
along the bathtub edge—the father, the
mother, the grandmother, the doctor, the
policeman, the child and the dog.

But each morning, when the sun came shining in on them, something would be different. The Tub Child would be standing between the Tub Mother and the Tub Father, their sides barely touching.

And if you looked very, very closely, you would see they all had smiles on their small wooden faces.

About My Tub People

BY PAM CONRAD

Pam Conrad

I remember two special tub people I had when I was a little girl. They were a man and a woman dancing. The man was gray with long pants and a tuxedo jacket. She was all pink with a long flowing skirt.

There was a window right over my bathtub, and if I stood up my chin would just reach the window sill. I would stand there, my feet in the warm soapy bathwater, and hold my dancing couple up to the window. From there we could see a train that ran past my house along the railroad tracks.

As the train rode past, the dancing man and woman would stand side by side and watch with me, their arms held out gracefully in front of them. But the minute the train was gone and I turned them towards each other, they would glide into each other's arms and begin waltzing.

When I sat back down in the tub, they would play with me. The soap my mother bought didn't float like my grandmother's soap did, so I would open the washcloth on top of the water for them to stand on.

Even today, so many years later, I can still hear my voice echoing in the green tiled bathroom as the waltzing woman would ask the waltzing man to watch her swim around their boat and warn her if he saw any sharks coming.

When I grew up and became a mother, my daughters had bathtub toys. There was a little mermaid and a dolphin, and a yellow duck, but I always loved the little wooden people best of all. There were parents, doctors, mailmen, firemen, teachers, children, and animals. When my girls were wrapped in towels and off to their bedrooms, I would line the wooden people up on the edge of the bathtub, to wait until the next day and the next bath.

Today, my daughters are nearly grown and they don't play with tub toys anymore. But on the bookshelf in my office I have saved a few of them, so that I can always remember. Can you guess which ones they are? Yes! There's a mother, a father, a grandmother, a doctor, a policeman, a child and a dog.

PULLING THE THEME TOGETHER

Adventure

1. The Tub People belong to you. Where have they been? Where will you have them go next?

2. Another adventure? Of course! Look back at what you have read in this book. You read about Pepito, Luke, a dinosaur family, the Tub People, and others. Choose one or two characters. Make a new adventure.

3. Find an adventure book. Find a good one. It can be fiction or nonfiction. Figure out how to make it sound exciting even to someone who says, "I have never read an adventure book."

BOOKS TO ENJOY

My Little Island
Written and illustrated by Frané Lessac

Three-foot-long lizards and giant barking frogs! These are some of the things a young boy and his friend see when they visit a Caribbean island.

The Tub Grandfather
by Pam Conrad
Illustrations by Richard Egielski

Join in and read the Tub People's newest adventure. In this story, the Tub child finds someone who has been missing for a very long time.

Department Store
Written and illustrated by Gail Gibbons

This book about department stores will show you places that most shoppers never see.

Wagon Wheels

by Barbara Brenner
Illustrations by Don Bolognese

The Muldie brothers must learn to
care for each other and be brave as
they travel across the wilderness.
Read about their adventure in this story
that really happened over a hundred years ago.

Guys from Space

Written and illustrated by Daniel Pinkwater

Would you take a ride with four green space guys?
The boy in this story does, but he has to be home
by six o'clock.

Gorilla

Written and illustrated by Anthony Browne

Hannah wants a real gorilla for her birthday,
not a toy one. Her father just doesn't
understand—or does he?

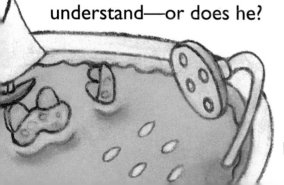

137

LITERARY TERMS

Characters

The people or animals in a story are called the **characters.** Sometimes we learn about a character through what other characters say. What did you learn about Pepito in *My Dog Is Lost?*

Fantasy

A story that *could not* happen in real life is a **fantasy.** *The Tub People* is a fantasy. Little wooden bathtub toys couldn't really talk or have feelings. What other fantasies have you read?

Nonfiction

Nonfiction tells facts about real people and things. Illustrations can help you understand nonfiction. The **labels** in some illustrations help you to understand the information.

sculptor

frame

Personification

Personification is the way an author makes toys or animals seem like people. The Tub People are wooden, but they act like real people when they smile, cry, and wink at each other.

Play

A **play** is a story that is written to be acted out. **Stage directions** are instructions that tell the characters what to do. In "Planet of the Grown-Ups," the stage directions tell the actor playing Zegna to shake everyone's hand.

Setting

Setting is where and when a story happens. In some stories, the setting changes. *The Lost Lake* begins in the city and ends in the mountains.

GLOSSARY

ad·ven·ture an unusual or exciting happening: *Flying in a jet is an adventure.* **adventures.**

back·pack a bag worn on the back by people hiking or going to school. *I filled my backpack with food for our camping trip.* **backpacks.**

car·ni·val a place of amusement with rides, games, and shows: *The carnival will be in town this weekend.* **carnivals.**

col·lec·tion a group of things that are from many places, but are brought together: *The stamps in his collection are from fifty different countries.* **collections.**

compass

com·pass something that shows directions. A compass has a needle that always points to the north: *We used our compass to get us out of the mountains.* **compasses.**

com·put·er a machine that can store and give back information. A computer can play games and give answers to problems: *Our class learns arithmetic on a computer.* **computers.**

con·duc·tor a person who helps the people who ride trains: *The conductor collects tickets and fares.* **conductors.**

computer

dis·cov·er·y a finding out; seeing or learning about something for the first time: *These fossils are an important discovery.* **discoveries.**

dis·play a showing or exhibit of items: *We saw a display of new books at the library.* **displays.**

Words from your stories

diz•zy   feeling that you are going to fall or spin around; not steady: *Looking down from a high place can make you dizzy.* **dizzier, dizziest.**

drain   a pipe for carrying off water or waste: *The bathtub drain is clogged.* **drains.**

ex•hib•it   **1.** to show in public: *She exhibited her paintings at the museum.* **2.** something shown in public: *I have an exhibit at the science fair.* **exhibited, exhibiting; exhibits.**

ex•pert   a person who has much skill or who knows a lot about a subject: *Corinne is an expert on rain forests.* **experts.**

fer•ry•boat   a boat that carries people and things across water: *The ferryboat carried the cars across the lake to the island.* **ferryboats.**

ferryboat

gasp   to take in a loud, quick breath of air; try hard to get your breath after running or working very hard: *The girl gasped after running all the way home from school.* **gasped, gasping.**

grown-up   a person who has finished growing; an adult: *A grown-up coaches the team.* **grown-ups.**

hike   **1.** to take a long walk: *We hiked five miles.* **2.** a long walk: *The campers went on a hike.* **hiked, hiking; hikes.**

hik•er   a person who goes on long walks: *Lee belongs to a hiker's club.* **hikers.**

hiker

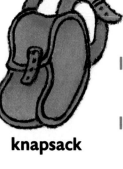

knapsack

knap•sack   a cloth bag for clothes or other items carried on the back: *If your knapsack is full, I can put your shoes in mine.* **knapsacks.**

lan•guage   words that people write or speak: *People in different countries sometimes speak and write different languages.* **languages.**

lone•ly   feeling sad because you are alone and need company: *He was lonely while his brother was away.* **lonelier, loneliest.**

mis•er•a•ble   very unhappy: *Khalid was miserable when his bike was stolen.*

out•doors•man   a man who spends much time outdoors: *A real outdoorsman loves to hike.* **outdoorsmen.**

out•doors•men   See **outdoorsman.**

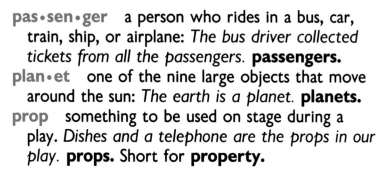

planet

pas•sen•ger   a person who rides in a bus, car, train, ship, or airplane: *The bus driver collected tickets from all the passengers.* **passengers.**

plan•et   one of the nine large objects that move around the sun: *The earth is a planet.* **planets.**

prop   something to be used on stage during a play. *Dishes and a telephone are the props in our play.* **props.** Short for **property.**

rap•ids   a part of a river where the water rushes quickly: *The boat was swept along by the rapids.*

sched•ule   a written or printed list of details or times: *Look in the newspaper for the movie schedule.* **schedules.**

sci•en•tist   a person who studies a science: *A scientist tries to find out why things are the way they are.* **scientists.**

search   to try to find something by looking for it: *We searched the house for Dad's car keys.* **searched, searching.**

shag•gy   covered with thick, rough hair or wool: *That coat is shaggy and very warm.* **shaggier, shaggiest.**

shaggy

sight   **1.** the power or sense of seeing. Sight is one of the five senses, along with hearing, smell, taste, and touch. **2.** something worth seeing: *The Grand Canyon is a beautiful sight.* **sights.**

skate•board   a board with roller-skate wheels at each end, used for gliding on a hard surface: *Beth rides a skateboard to school.* **skateboards.**

spe•cial ef•fect   way of creating a sound or a sight on stage and in movies: *The special effects in the film made the spaceship seem to explode.* **special effects.**

sta•tion   a place used for a special reason, or where you can get a special service: *You can buy your ticket at the train station.* **stations.**

sub•way   an underground electric railroad. Subways run beneath the surface of the streets in a city: *Morrie liked to travel on the subway.* **subways.**

trav•el•er   a person who travels: *The plane was full of summer travelers.* **travelers.**

vis•i•tor   a person who visits; guest: *Our visitors will stay with us for a week.* **visitors.**

whirl•pool   a current of water whirling around and around quickly. *There was a small whirlpool just below the waterfall.* **whirlpools.**

wink

wink   to quickly close and open one eye as a hint or signal: *I winked at my sister when it was time to leave.* **winked, winking.**

143

ACKNOWLEDGMENTS

Text

Page 6: *My Dog Is Lost* by Ezra Jack Keats and Pat Cherr. Copyright © 1960 by HarperCollins Publishers. Reprinted by permission of HarperCollins Publishers.

Page 36: *The Lost Lake* by Allen Say. Copyright © 1989 by Allen Say. Reprinted by permission of Houghton Mifflin Company.

Page 54: "Songs of the Horse Society," by Frances Densmore, *Teton Sioux Music.* Bureau of American Ethnology Bulletin 61. Washington, 1918.

Page 56: "Dinosaurs on the Road," from *Dinosaurs Travel: A Guide for Families on the Go* by Laurie Krasny Brown and Marc Brown. Copyright © 1988 by Laurie Krasny Brown and Marc Brown. By permission of Little, Brown and Company.

Page 78: From *Dinosaurs, Dragonflies and Diamonds: All About Natural History Museums* by Gail Gibbons. Copyright © 1988 by Gail Gibbons. Reprinted by permission of Four Winds Press, an imprint of Macmillan Publishing Company.

Page 98: "Learning About Natural History Museums," by Gail Gibbons. Copyright © by Gail Gibbons, 1991.

Page 102: "Planet of the Grown-Ups," by Gus Gedatus. Copyright © by Gus Gedatus, 1991.

Page 116: "Summer Song" by John Ciardi from *The Man Who Sang the Sillies.* Copyright ©1961 by John Ciardi. Reprinted by permission of the Estate of John Ciardi.

Page 118: *The Tub People* by Pam Conrad. Illustrated by Richard Egielski. Text copyright © 1989 by Pam Conrad. Illustrations copyright © 1989 by Richard Egielski. Reprinted by permission of HarperCollins Publishers.

Page 132: "About My Tub People," afterword for *The Tub People* by Pam Conrad. Copyright © 1991 by Pam Conrad. Reprinted by permission of Maria Carvainis Agency, Inc.

Artists

Illustrations owned and copyrighted by the illustrator.
Lee Lee Brazeal, cover, 1–5, 135–144
Ezra Jack Keats and Pat Cherr, 6–35
Allen Say, 36–53
Debbie Drechsler, 54–55
Laurie Krasny Brown and Marc Brown, 56–77
Gail Gibbons, 78–101
Marc Rosenthal, 102–115
Craig Smallish, 116–117
Richard Egielski, 118–134

Photographs

Unless otherwise acknowledged, all photographs are the property of Scott Foresman.
Page 99: Courtesy of Gail Gibbons
Page 133: Courtesy of Pam Conrad

Glossary

The contents of this glossary have been adapted from *My Second Picture Dictionary,* Copyright © 1990 Scott, Foresman and Company and *Beginning Dictionary,* Copyright © 1988 Scott, Foresman and Company.